MANUAL OF INSTRUCTIONS

CW01471666

A Group or Individual

Word Recognition Test

(for the early stages: up to about 8 years 6 months)

Clifford Carver

Formerly Associate Professor,
Department of Educational Psychology,
University of Manitoba, Canada

HODDER AND STOUGHTON
LONDON SYDNEY AUCKLAND TORONTO

ISBN 0 340 11776 1

Printed in Great Britain for
Hodder and Stoughton Educational,
a division of Hodder and Stoughton Ltd,
Mill Road, Dunton Green, Sevenoaks, Kent,
by Chigwell Press, Buckhurst Hill, Essex.

Contents

Aims

The *Word Recognition Test*, which can be group or individually administered, is designed to give the teacher two assessments of a child's word recognition ability:

a. the child's *overall* level of ability in word recognition which is provided by the child's total correct score on the test;

b. an analysis of the child's *errors and difficulties* in word recognition, achieved by a close study of the type of correct and incorrect responses made by the child.

Brief description of the Word Recognition Test

The test comprises 50 items. Each item consists of a row of words, one word of which is the correct answer. *The stimulus word is given orally by the teacher, or administrator,* and the child is asked to select and underline the correct word (stimulus word) in each row.

The test assesses word recognition (not "conceptual" reading in the sense of comprehension) from the earliest stages of letter knowledge to a level normally achieved at about 8 years 6 months. The test is constructed differently from the normal word list type of test, and though a child may know a word in its normal context, he may find difficulty in deciding the answer when the same word is presented within a structured group of alternatives. It is these difficulties that the *Word Recognition Test* illuminates.

The items are arranged in generally increasing order of difficulty. Normally the child would be required to attempt the whole 50 items.

General instructions

1. The child will require only a pencil. Spares should be available. Children should be well spaced out to prevent "copying". A whole class is usually found to be a convenient size for administration. The test is untimed, but would usually take from 15 to 30 minutes to administer. A general rule should be that the younger, more retarded,

2

and less sophisticated the children, the smaller would be the group. With adequate supervision large numbers of children could be tested.

An assistant in the room is desirable with younger children. The assistant's role is to ensure that the children:

a. understand the method of answering,
b. are not losing their place on the paper,
c. are not falling behind.

2. It is essential that an atmosphere of cheerfulness and friendliness is established with the younger children. The "puzzle" element should be stressed. It should be pointed out that the child will not be reading, that the *answer* will be given by the teacher and that the children are to puzzle out which is the *right* answer. With a non-stressful atmosphere, with patience, and with small groups, children of 4-5 years who have some knowledge of word recognition can be assessed. If necessary, the test can be given with breaks, say at the end of each page.

3. If productive information is to be acquired the children should be encouraged to try each item, guessing if necessary. However, the teacher should avoid giving hints to an individual child, such as telling him to "look again", when he has made an error. The children should be *discouraged* from impulsively selecting a word, and *encouraged* to look at each word in the row before underlining.

Though the children should be encouraged to try, over-anxiety should be avoided. In exceptional cases, where a young child is upset his test should be abandoned if necessary, and assessment carried out individually.

Where a child is clearly a non-reader, this will quickly be seen during the first 10 items. The test can then be abandoned since no diagnosis of letter ability is possible other than that the child has none. (He can be quietly told to do the drawing of a man on the inside of the cover.)

4. Inside the cover is a page on which the child will be asked to draw a man. This drawing can be carried out at the end of the test as a relaxing reward. The children should be encouraged to draw a big man. This drawing gives a rough indication of the child's motor or visuo/motor ability.

5. Fill in the cover details—the child's name, date of birth, chronological age, sex, and the date of administration.

Working the practice item on the cover

The aim of the practice item is to ensure that all the children understand the very simple method of answering. No calling out should be allowed throughout the test.

Copy on to the blackboard the words:

man   dog   boy   girl   cat

Have the children put a finger below the figure 1 on the cover. Tell the children:

"In the box you will see five words like mine on the blackboard. You don't have to read the words but I want you to look at each one. Do that. Put your finger on each word and look at each word. Now I'm going to say one of the words and I want to see if you can find it. When you have found it put your finger under the word. Ready!

The word is . . . CAT . . . Find cat.

A cat chases mice.

Find . . . CAT . . . and put your finger under it.

A cat chases mice.

If you can't find . . . CAT . . . guess the one you think it *might* be."

(CHECK)

"Who has found CAT?

Good, now look at the blackboard.

Who thinks it is this one?" (Point to *man*.)

"Who thinks it is this one?" (Point to *dog*, then *boy*, then *girl*.)

"Who thinks it is this one?" (Point to *cat*.)

"Good, that's the right one, so we put a line under it. Put a line under *cat*, like this." (Underline on blackboard.)

(CHECK)

"Look at the blackboard again." (Rub out the line under *cat* and draw a line under *dog*.)

"Suppose I put the line under this instead of *cat*. Is that right? No, so I will cross out the line, like this, and put it under *cat*."

(man   d̶o̶g̶   boy   girl   <u>cat</u>)

NOTE: The stimulus word, throughout, is given separately and also in a meaningful sentence. This enables the child to *internalise* the word, and to relate it to his own pronunciation. This is especially useful with children having speech defects or deafness. The word (*cat*) should be given *clearly but without undue emphasis on elements within the word*. The stimulus word and the sentence (or phrase) may be given two or three times. In the sentence the stimulus word can be lightly emphasised.

DO NOT TRY TO TEACH THE WORD OR THE LETTERS OF THE WORD DURING THE TEST.
Tell the children you are now going to let them try some more words without any help.

The test proper

Write the figures 1 to 10 clearly, downwards, on the blackboard. Have the children open the booklet and fold back the cover. Ensure they have the booklet open on the page with *one star* at the top. Have the children identify the first box. (Point to figure 1 on the blackboard.)

Explain that you will give the word; that they should look at each word in box 1; that when they think they have found the word, they are to put a line under it. Remind them that if they make a mistake and put a line under the wrong word, they can cross out the wrong line and put it under another word. Give the word and sentence (or phrase) two or three times if necessary. Remind the children at the start of a new page how to correct a wrong answer.

Tell the children:

"Put your finger on the box with number 1 in it.

Look at the row of words in the box.

I want you to find . . . ORANGE . . . Look at all the words in the box. Find . . . ORANGE . . . *Orange that we eat.* When you have found it, put a line under it. Put a line under . . . ORANGE . . . *Orange that we eat.*" (Avoid blurring the stimulus word when giving it as a separate word, e.g. "underlineorange".) "When you have done that, put your finger on number 2; put your finger on the next box with number 2 in it." (Point to figure 2 on the blackboard.)

All the items in the test are treated similarly. The first page will be taken more slowly. Though the children should not be rushed through the test, unnecessary lingering can cause fatigue and restlessness. Each page is "starred" with one, two, three, four, or five stars.

Only one page should be dealt with at a time. This prevents distraction and also avoids the slower child worrying about the apparent mass of words to be read. The children should be instructed to fold the booklet in half down the centre. Have them identify the number of stars at the top of the page. Items are numbered 1 to 10 on the left-hand side of each page, and also 1 to 50 (in small figures on the right) for the teacher's convenience.

A break can be given for younger children at the end of ** page.

At the end of the test, have the children fold the booklet to show the blank page inside the cover. Tell them:

"Now you can draw a man on this page. Make him big. Fill the page. Try to draw a really good big man."

Stimulus words and sentences (or phrases)

The word in capitals is given as a discrete word, and also given in the sentence (or phrase).

★ 1. ORANGE that we eat (1)
2. we went TO the park (2)
3. LOOK at the words, said . . . (3)
4. the girl played with a TOY (4)
5. ASHES in the fire (5)
6. PIG in a pigsty (6)
7. INKPOT with ink in it (7)
8. CHIN on your face (8)
9. the boy had JAM on his fingers (9)
10. he WAS playing in the park (10)

(*At the end of each page, ensure that the children fold back the page, that they identify the next page with the correct number of stars at the top, and that they identify the box with figure 1 in it. If necessary, point to the figure 1 on the blackboard.*)

★★ 1. the FOX was in the wood (11)
2. JUST a moment said . . . (12)
3. give it to ME, said . . . (13)
4. GRASS is green (14)
5. come WITH me said . . . (15)
6. you are a BAD boy said . . . (16)
7. WHEN are you coming home, said . . . (17)
8. SHOP, where we buy things
(alternative: I SHOP at the store with . . .) (18)
9. where HAS it gone, said . . . (19)
10. HER mother came to meet them (20)

★★★ 1. a LOUD noise (21)
2. the FROG in a pond (22)
3. she MET her mother in the street (23)
4. a piece OF chocolate (24)
5. the PEN on the desk (25)
6. the fire began to BURN (26)
7. LICK your lollipops (27)
8. the little girl PLAYED with her toys (28)
9. a piece of CAKE (29)
10. the cowboy had a GUN (30)

****
1. she SAW her mother at the window (31)
2. the BUS was full of people (32)
3. the mouse was in the TRAP (33)
4. a BOAT sailing on the sea (34)
5. go to your PLACE said teacher (35)
6. the judge put on his WIG (36)
7. ten and ten make TWENTY (37)
8. the girl had a RED face (38)
9. it was a dark NIGHT (39)
10. POST the letter, please . . .
(alternative: I mail my letters at the POST office) (40)

*****
1. the aeroplane had a broken WING (41)
2. this is for YOU said . . . (42)
3. she was standing in the RAIN (43)
4. the old man was tired, his head began to NOD (44)
5. Polly put the KETTLE on (45)
6. a BIRD in the sky (46)
7. be QUIET please said . . . (47)
8. don't SPLASH water on me (48)
9. this PART is for you said . . . (49)
10. WHO are you she said (50)

N.B. The dots (e.g. said . . .) indicate that the end of the phrase or sentence is left open for appropriate completions such as: "said daddy", "said her mother", "said the teacher".
The stars indicate the page number on which each set of 10 items is located.

The alternative sentences for items 18 and 40 are for use in North America. The *Word Recognition Test* has been used extensively in Canada, and a recent survey in Calgary among fairly representative children from Grades I and II yielded the following results.

	NO.	AVERAGE AGE	MEAN SCORE	PREDICTED LEVEL FROM NORMS (p.8)
Grade I	147	6y 9¼m	36·1	6y 9m
Grade II	144	7y 10½m	45·4	8y 0m

Norms

SCORE	W.R. AGE		STAGES*
0–9			1
10–14	4y	0m	2
15–16	4y	3m	
17–18	4y	6m	3
19–20	4y	9m	
21–22	5y	0m	4
23–24	5y	3m	
25–26	5y	6m	5
27–28	5y	9m	
29–30	6y	0m	6
31–32	6y	3m	
33–34	6y	6m	7
35–36	6y	9m	
37–38	7y	0m	8
39–40	7y	3m	
41–42	7y	6m	9
†43–44	7y	9m	
45–46	8y	0m	
47–48	8y	3m	10
49–50	8y	6m *and above*	

Scores grouped at three monthly intervals (i.e. 13, 14 = 4y 0m) to avoid unreal exactness in giving the child a precise age level.

*Stages (see page 16): scores are more coarsely grouped to form ten stages of word recognition.

†Mean score of 1005 children at average chronological age 7y 9m.

Marking

The child is credited with one mark for each word correctly underlined.

If the child has made an alteration, or his intention is *clear*, mark accordingly. If the child had underlined the correct word *and* another (without making his intention clear), count the *error* as the answer. (This is for diagnosis of errors.) If two or more incorrect words are underlined in the row, count as no response.

Count up *all* the child's correct answers and note the total on the cover under the *Word Recognition Test* score. Refer to the table of norms (page 8) and translate the score to an age level norm.

Background of the test

The *Word Recognition Test* items were part of an extensive battery of 300 test items which were used to investigate aural (sound) and visual factors in word recognition. The subtests, given in Appendix II (page 23), included "Non Letter tests" (visual perception, rhymes and initial sounds), and Letter and Picture tests. The statistical details of correlations, etc., are given in this appendix. This initial analysis enabled it to be proved whether, and to what degree, a multiple choice word recognition test (as used here) did actually assess word recognition.

The *Word Recognition Test* reveals not only the child's knowledge of the visual aspects of letters and words, but also his ability to hear and analyse sounds themselves. For example, one child may be familiar with the visual shape of the letter *c* in "cat" (or with the visual aspect of the word "cat") without being able to hear any of the sounds of which "cat" is composed. Another child may be able to distinguish the sounds in "cat" without having had any teaching of the visual aspect of letters. An error made by a child in reading a word could be due to visual and/or aural causes.

The aural analysis of words is held here to be the more crucial prerequisite for word recognition.

By using a multiple choice method in the *Word Recognition Test* (i.e. selecting one word from several), the child is presented with *systematic and structured alternatives, alongside the correct answer*. This means that in addition to the types of word correctly answered by the child, *the types of error made can also be assessed*.

By careful design of the alternatives and by statistical analysis of each item (see page 12) a selection of items was made that would give information regarding the child's ability (aurally and/or visually) in manipulating letters and words. Though every item does not include every type of error, the test as a whole covers the following:

a. Initial letter errors (consonants and vowels) (e.g. *a*range for *o*range; *b*ook for *l*ook)

b. Distortion or twisting of letters (e.g. *y*am for *j*am; *q*en for *p*en)

c. Mid-vowel errors (e.g. m*i*t for m*e*t)

d. Serial distortion of letters (e.g. *aws* for *was*)

e. Reversal of words (e.g. *giw* for *wig*)

f. Errors in common word-endings (e.g. *cak* for *cake*)

g. Initial multiple consonant errors (e.g. *t*ap for *tr*ap; *l*ace for *pl*ace)

h. "Combined vowel" errors (e.g. p*or*t for p*ar*t; b*i*d for b*ir*d)

i. Regular (phonic) and irregular (sight) words (e.g. red; who)

For convenience the back page of the test is arranged so that errors can be conveniently classed under these headings. A more detailed explanation of the diagnosis of errors will be given later.

For general interest the following were, in order, the five major factors which arose from the original battery of tests (Appendix II), and which could reasonably be accepted as influencing word recognition and hence were reflected in the *Word Recognition Test:*

a. interaction of aural and visual abilities;

b. ability to organise a series of visual symbols;

c. ability to analyse sounds (aurally);

d. comprehension of spoken language;

e. sex (i.e. boys tend to have more disability than girls).

These factors should be taken into account when devising educational programmes especially for retarded readers. Non-reading activities which develop the child's ability in the first four factors would be reflected in improved word recognition.

Analysis of the items in the test

Every item in the larger battery was statistically analysed. Before final item selection, intercorrelations and factorial analyses were also carried out. A brief explanation will be given here, while for those interested Appendix I gives full details of sample used, item facility, and discrimination.

ITEM FACILITY

Facility (F) is a simple measure of the total percentage of the whole sample of children answering the item correctly. For example, an item of 20 per cent Facility would be "difficult" while one of 90 per cent Facility would be "easy".

Though the items are generally in increasing order of difficulty (decreasing Facility), the main body of the items was selected to reflect a level of ability around the age of 6 to 6½ years, this being the crucial area of the early stages of word recognition, and the area where accurate information is most needed. Easier and more difficult items (22 items) were added to extend the range of the test, to ensure greater reliability, and to give the children at the very early stages an introduction to the test.

DISCRIMINATION

The discrimination of each item was calculated before selection. The items finally selected ranged from a discrimination of ·60 to ·94.

Discrimination means the degree to which an item differentiates the more able word "recognisers" from the less able, regardless of the overall Facility of that item. For example, a high discrimination item consistently shows more and more children failing the item as one moves down the scale of word recognition ability. In other words, items of high discrimination are more reliable than those of low discrimination.

Below (A) is shown an actual item which has a very high discrimination, and an item (B) of *similar overall difficulty* which was rejected because of lower discrimination.

Percentage of group answering correctly

(A)

Ability in Word Recognition			
Top 1/6th	93%	88% Top 1/3rd	
2 1/6th	82%		
3 1/6th	71%		
4 1/6th	52%		
5 1/6th	25%	17% Bottom 1/3rd	
Bottom 1/6th	8%		

Facility 56% Discrimination 71% (88% - 17%)

(B)

Top 1/6th	90%	77% Top 1/3rd
2 1/6th	59%	
3 1/6th	75%	
4 1/6th	48%	
5 1/6th	33%	27% Bottom 1/3rd
Bottom 1/6th	21%	

Facility 55% Discrimination 50% (77% - 27%)

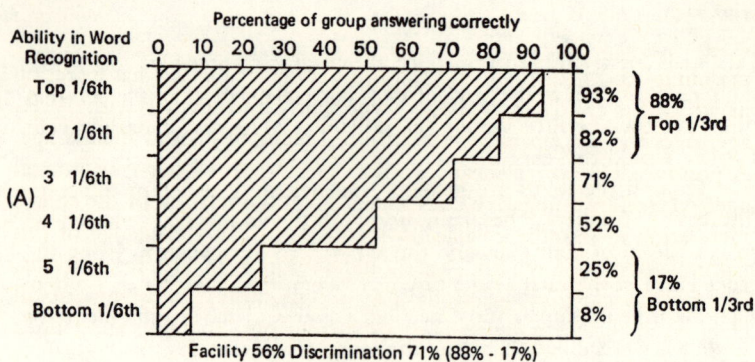

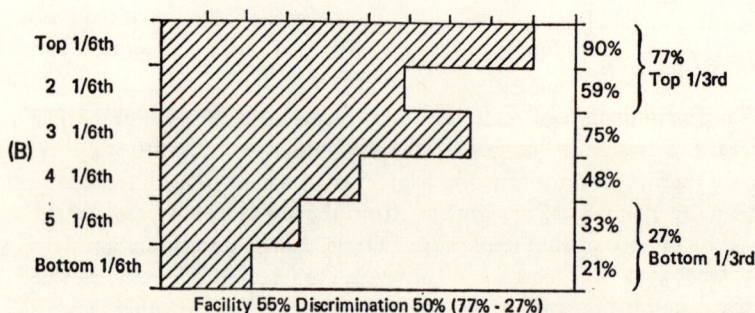

EXAMPLES OF TWO ITEMS OF SIMILAR DIFFICULTY (*Facility*)
a.   Suitable item accepted (wig: item 36)
b.   Rejected item

Uses of the test

The group administration, together with the norms and diagnostic uses, makes the *Word Recognition Test* useful in a variety of ways.
a.   For *large scale assessments*—these would be used either to identify reading problems or simply as periodic surveys.
b.   For *screening* by clinics or remedial centres—this enables "office desk" decisions to be made regarding utilisation of remedial education facilities. The establishing of a child's mental age (by a good non-verbal

reasoning test) helps here and the front cover of the test has a section in which the child's mental age is entered. This together with W.R. age gives the discrepancy between word recognition and mental age. A positive discrepancy means word recognition is higher than mental age; conversely a negative discrepancy gives the relation of the child's retardation in months, relative to mental age. The knowledge of this form of retardation is useful, but should be employed with reservations.

c.   For *school records*—periodic (say six monthly) assessment of all children at the early stages is easily carried out, enabling the child's rate of progress to be evaluated.

d.   For *research*—this is a fruitful area for such a test since the errors made by a child or by groups of children can be scored quantitatively. In research the use of raw scores, rather than word recognition ages, would be recommended.

e.   For *diagnostic use*—one of the most interesting and valuable aspects of the *Test* is in its diagnosis of perceptual errors in word recognition.

DIAGNOSTIC USE

Further research showed that the child "learns" letters in a rather more regular and systematic pattern than might be expected—that not only do "letters" present varying degrees of visual difficulties in a predictable system, but that letters have a system of difficulty also in the aural field. As previously stated, it is concluded here that it is not in the visual perceptual field that the major difficulty in word recognition lies, but in the aural perceptual field—specifically in the analysis of sounds themselves.

It is the interacting of a child's visual and aural organisation that is reflected as "letter knowledge". A close analysis of a child's pattern of answers on the *Word Recognition Test* enables a diagnosis (to a lesser or greater degree) to be made of his difficulties with letters, this letter difficulty being the overt reflection of his perceptual experiences and failures.

A child's physical state in visual acuity and especially in hearing acuity should always be known. Audiometric tests should also include assessment of high or low frequency deafness, since the frequencies within words vary greatly. A child may be unable to learn the letter *s* because he cannot hear it. The detrimental effect on the child's development of speech, language, comprehension and concepts is self evident. Though many other factors—for example, social, emotional, and personality—affect a child's attitude to reading and learning, it is the perceptual errors which concern us here, for failure in "perception" means failure in word recognition.

By studying the answer pattern on the *Word Recognition Test* an assessment of the child's perceptual difficulties can be made. Treatment and methods can then be much more surely constructed, leading either to a more thorough individual diagnostic assessment, or to enlightened guidance which takes into account the child's difficulties.

Diagnosis should take into account four broad areas:

a.   the child's chronological age;
b.   the child's general word recognition level (age norm);
c.   the child's pattern of correct responses;
d.   the child's pattern of errors among the multiple choices.

Chronological age: Visual abilities mature much earlier than aural abilities. Thus a young child—say, below 8 years—should not be expected to have reached a complete aural organisation, whereas a 12-year-old, who from his answers might be thought to be confusing *sounds* themselves, would be quite a different problem, possibly having a severe disability which would warrant a detailed physical or neurological examination.

General level (age norm): A child whose general level is, say, less than 5 years (below a score of 21) would still be preoccupied with initial letters and their serial aspect. This would be his *general* stage reached, while a child at, say, a level of 7 years (a score of about 37), who had made occasional errors in initial letters (e.g. "lace" for "place"), or in serial orientation (say, "giw" for "wig"), might have a difficulty which warranted specific attention.

Pattern of correct responses: A list of the correct responses made by the child might be drawn up. Each item would then be studied to arrive at an assumption of what the child knows. For example, item 28 requires the child to select the word *played* from among the following choices:

ployed   day   ball   played   pliyed

Assuming the correct response is made by the child (*played*), it does not mean that he necessarily understands the structure of the word "played". Nor does it mean that he knows the initial consonants *pl*. It does imply that he

—knows the initial letter *p* (not having chosen "day" or "ball", i.e. *d* or *b*, for *p*),

—perhaps knows *pl* (since knowing *p*, his choice must result in one of the *pl* alternatives),

—very likely knows the structure of *ay* (not having chosen "ball", "ployed", or pliyed").

These are still, of course, assumptions, since on any single item the child could be making a random guess. More important, it should be seen that though the child might, from his answer, be reasonably judged as able to hear and discriminate the *sound p*, no opportunity is given in this item to confuse *p* with *q* (its nearest coʒfusion) *visually*. The confusion of *p* and *b is* allowed for in this item (by "ball").

A study of all the child's correct responses (together with his general level) will reveal the word recognition structures known by the child. The odd difficult item, correctly chosen by a child with a low score, will easily be detected as random guessing. Again, a child with a moderate score may guess a rather difficult word correctly. This will usually indicate more than a random shot in the dark.

Study of errors: A similar close study of the child's error choices might be made. For example, in item 41 the child is asked to choose the word *wing* from the following:

weng   wung   wig   wag   wing

Here the child cannot make an initial error. He could be uncertain of, or not know, the ending *ng*, resulting in a choice of "wig" or "wag". If the child had already shown knowledge of initial letters (from analysis of his correct responses), then the error choice of "wig" would probably represent lack of knowledge of *ng*; the choice of "wag" could indicate a similar failure *plus* uncertainty of vowel sounds. The choice of "wung" or "weng" would very likely indicate vowel confusions. Where sufficient evidence is available, it is possible to infer from these letter errors whether the confusion is likely to be aural (most likely among the higher levels of ability), or visual (frequent at the earlier stages, but perhaps also having a basis of aural difficulty).

If the test is well administered, and the child is encouraged to study the whole of the series in an item before deciding on his answer, a very comprehensive set of inferences can often be made. The child who is making random guesses is easily detected. However, this is rare, since what happens is that a child is not guessing randomly, but guessing from rudimentary knowledge.

To assist the teacher, the *broad structures* of word recognition expected at various levels, are listed in the table on pages 16-18. Though this table is based on very exacting research, the details should not be followed slavishly, since the results are statistical averages of abilities and stages, and would not necessarily apply in the same detail individually.

By making a diagnosis using chronological age, word recognition level, correct structures and failings in word recognition, by studying the results in relation to the table of stages, by inferring whether the disabilities are visual, aural, or both, and by using other information often readily available to the teacher (for example, non-verbal and other abilities), the treatment of an individual child can be planned on a very sound basis.

It would be wise to refer any child whose word recognition age is two years behind his chronological age to an agency such as a Child Guidance Clinic. Young children who are showing little or no structural knowledge of letters should be carefully observe since this is likely to be an indication of later trouble.

Bizarre answers (confusing or distorting of letters and words, underlining every word in the row, underlining the first word in every row and so on) should also alert the teacher to the possibility that these are symptomatic of difficulties requiring further diagnosis.

Finally, it is useful, if possible, to observe the child's attitude and approach during the test. This would include whether a child was over-anxious, or careless; whether a child was constantly changing his mind about answers; or whether a child was extremely slow in his responses.

Table of general stages in word recognition

	APPROXIMATE LEVEL OF WORD RECOGNITION ABILITY	SCORES	GENERAL STAGE INDICATED
I	Below 4 years	Below 10	Virtually no word recognition knowledge. (If the child is over 7 years, severe difficulties are indicated, such as probable neurological disability in hearing sounds. There may also be some motor disability. A thorough diagnosis should be made and the child's physical state investigated.)

APPROXIMATE LEVEL OF WORD RECOGNITION ABILITY	SCORES	GENERAL STAGE INDICATED
2 Below 4½ years	10-16	Knowledge rudimentary; may have knowledge of a few initial letters, especially some initial short vowels, and perhaps *c, m, w, r, f, t.*
3 4½-5 years	17-20	Cannot assume child has insight into serial aspects of letters; cannot assume aural discrimination of sound; some initial letter/sounds known, but not all; may be at stage of hearing initial letter in words such as *c*amel but not in *c*limb.
4 5-5½ years	21-24	Probably somewhat more than half initial letters known; can also relate a few simple consonants at the end of words; easier short vowels (*o, a*) probably known in words; serial aspect of letters may still be weak.
5 5½-6 years	25-28	Most of initial letters now identified; accelerated increase in knowledge of word endings; still likely to be confused over nuances between short vowel sounds *e, i, u.*
6 6-6½ years	29-32	Practically all initial sounds heard and visually identified, though may still have difficulty with initial letters such as *q, v, h, p, b.* More or less able to identify short vowel sounds and associate the visual letters; may still have a few confusions regarding initial position of letters (serial aspect).
7 6½-7 years	33-36	Beginning to discriminate aurally initial multiple consonants (e.g. *cl, gr, fl*); probably recognises simpler ones (such as *pl, fr*) in

APPROXIMATE LEVEL OF WORD RECOGNITION ABILITY	SCORES	GENERAL STAGE INDICATED
7 6½-7 years *(cont.)*	33-36	words; could still be confusing *b* and *d*; strong knowledge of the initial sound, its equivalent letter symbol and its serial position at the left of a word; could still have a specific vowel discrimination difficulty, especially with short *i* and *e*, and possibly *u*; most single letter endings identified.
8 7-7½ years	37-40	Growing command of initial multiple consonants (especially *bl, pr, fr, br*); may still have difficulty in "hearing" (revealed by difficulty in discriminating aurally between, say, *cl, gl, cr, gr*.)
9 7½-8 years	41-44	More sophisticated learning, e.g. of the combined vowel sounds *or, aw*; generally knows and hears initial consonants *ch* and *th*, though may have difficulty in discriminating between *ch* and *sh*; initial multiple consonants well established, including *sw, ch, gl, cr, th, dr, gr*; developing ability to discriminate initial letter *s* together with a second consonant, but may be limited to *sc* and *sw*.
10 8 plus years	45 and over	A thorough knowledge of the double initial consonants now established; probably all simple single letter endings known. Simpler endings such as *ing* established; beginning to conquer *st, sl, sn, sm, sp*; insight into *th tw* (initially); manipulating groups such as *ar, ow, oy*, but complex initial groups yet to be conquered (*spr, str, thr*), and difficult endings such as *ch, sh*; recognition of difficult groups such as *ir, er, ur*, developing.

CORRECT COMPLETION OF THE TEST

If the child has confidently and correctly answered all the items in the *Word Recognition Test*, it can be assumed that a sound structural basis to word recognition has developed. Learning now becomes more sophisticated. Much information has to be gained from the context, and progress depends on the child's vocabulary, experience, success, fluency and intelligence. Alternatives have to be judged. For example, the child has to assess the possible sound of *s* given to the letter *c* (in "ceiling").

However, it can generally be assumed that the child's aural perception has matured sufficiently for further progress to be made. In the exceptional case, individual help should prove successful since the child's recognition of words is now based on knowledge, not simply on intuitive guessing.

Reliability, validity and standardisation

Both during and after construction of the *Word Recognition Test* intensive statistical studies were carried out to confirm:

a.   whether the results from the test were reliable;
b.   whether a test of this nature actually *was* measuring the child's ability to recognise words;
c.   whether norms could be included in addition to the diagnostic aims of the test.

RELIABILITY

Technical details of reliability tests are provided, in summary form, in Appendix II (page 23).

VALIDITY

Factorial studies were carried out on the original battery (from which the final items were selected), and on the final version of the test. These validity studies included comparisons with the *Burt (Rearranged) Word Reading Test*, the *Schonell Graded Word Reading Test*, alphabetical knowledge tests, vowel tests, visual perception tests, rhyming tests, independent word lists, and so on. The children involved in these investigations included retarded readers as well as normal children. These results are also summarised in Appendix II.

STANDARDISATION

Before deciding on the form of standardisation provided on page 8, four aspects of the *Word Recognition Test* were specially studied: *a.* its relationship to both the Burt and the Schonell tests; *b.* its upper level; *c.* distribution of median scores; *d.* relationship between median score and chronological age.

a. The relationship of the *Word Recognition Test* to both the Burt and the Schonell tests was first ascertained. These latter tests, involving the reading of a list of words, were standardised over a wide age range of children. The Burt test purports to have a basal age level of 4 years; the basal age level of the Schonell test is given as 5 years.

The correlation between the final *Word Recognition Test* scores of the 79 junior children in the original sample and their scores on the Schonell test was ·90 (see page 23). The correlation between the *Word Recognition Test* scores and the Burt reading test scores of the 168 children used in the validation study was ·823 (see page 24). Despite the restricted age ranges and levels of ability in these two samples, an extremely close relationship was found between the *Word Recognition Test* and the two other reading measures.

b. In the original sample, the children within the Schonell Reading Age interval 8y 2m to 8y 9m obtained a median *Word Recognition Test* score of 48, the median Reading Age for children scoring 47 to 50 being 8y 6m. The results from the Burt testing showed that the children in the Burt Reading Age group 8y 2m to 8y 6m had a median *Word Recognition Test* score of 48, the median Reading Age of the group scoring 48 to 50 again being 8y 6m. The 130 children in the final sample of 1005 children in the *chronological* age interval 8y 4m to 8y 7m obtained a median *Word Recognition Test* score of 48.

It was therefore concluded with some confidence that the upper level of the *Word Recognition Test* could be set at about $8\frac{1}{2}$ years.

c. A study of the distribution of median scores of the children aged 7y 0m to 8y 7m in the final sample showed a reasonably steady progression.

Median WRT scores	35	37	42	44	48
Chronological ages	7y 0m–	7y 4m–	7y 8m–	8y 0m–	8y 4m–
	7y 3m	7y 7m	7y 11m	8y 3m	8y 7m

d. The median score of the 1005 children in the final sample was 43, the mean age being 7y 9m. A line was drawn from the established theoretical upper limit through the median score and extended downwards.

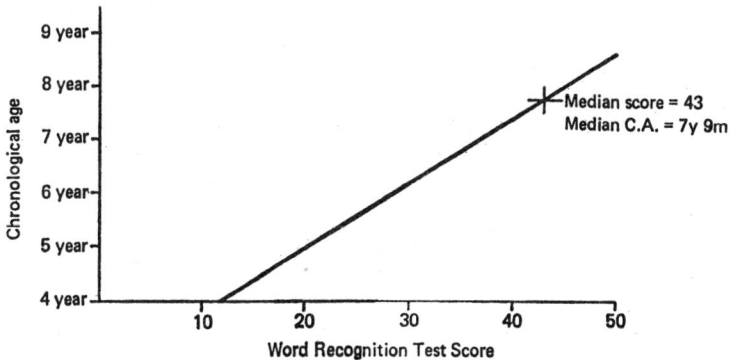

It can be seen that a score of 12 on the *Word Recognition Test* yields an age level of 4 years. This was remarkably close to the median score of 11 obtained by the children in the age group 4y 0m to 4y 4m in the original sample.

The use of an exact age norm is very suspect at the early stages of word recognition. The overt score provided by the correct "reading" of a few simple words is merely *some* reflection of the complex process taking place within the child. It is not until an age level of about 6½ years that a reading "norm" begins to have some reality. However, unless a test of word recognition differentiates among children at the early stages, the young retarded reader is unlikely to be identified. That is, if the lowest norm of a test be set at 6½ years, then the 7-year-old child could be at the most only 6 months retarded.

The *Word Recognition Test* was designed to be particularly sensitive at the early stages of word recognition. In view of the findings outlined above, it was decided for practical purposes to accept that word recognition was a steady linear growth. Scores and ages were grouped to avoid an unreal exactness of age level, and these are provided on page 8. To obtain a more marked appreciation of retardation among very young children, the norms can be extended downwards to provide statistical levels of, say, 3y 6m and 3y 9m.

Original sample, item facility, item discrimination

SAMPLE

148 children (60 per cent boys, 40 per cent girls)
Full range of infant children 6–7 years
Lower half of junior children (7–9 years in reading ability)
Remedial class of 7, 8 and 9 years
Mean chronological age 7·8 years (SD 1·0 years)
Mean reading age (Schonell) 6·9 years (SD 1·4 years)
Mean IQ (*Moray House Picture Test*) 101·3 (SD 13·7)

ORIGINAL TRY-OUT BATTERY

Scores	0/9	10/19	20/29	30/39	40/49	50/59	60/69	70/79	80/89	90 and over
Frequency	1	3	16	12	19	14	17	10	21	35

Distribution of raw scores
Mean score 63·9 (SD 25·6)

FINAL TEST

Scores	0/5	6/10	11/15	16/20	21/25	26/30	31/35	36/40	41/45	46/50
Frequency	2	9	17	20	13	15	9	10	15	38

Distribution of raw scores on the final selection of 50 items
Mean score 30·8 (SD 14·2)
Median score 29·3

FACILITY OF FINAL ITEMS

%F of items	30%/39%	40%/49%	50%/59%	60%/69%	70%/79%	80%/89%
Frequency	4	7	10	13	10	6

Mean F = 62%

DISCRIMINATION OF FINAL TEST ITEMS

Discrimination	·60–·69	·70–·79	·80–·89	·90–1·0
Frequency	15	26	8	1

Reliability and validity studies

COMPARATIVE CORRELATIONS EXTRACTED FROM BATTERY OF TESTS
ADMINISTERED TO THE 148 CHILDREN FOR THE CONSTRUCTION OF THE
WORD RECOGNITION TEST

Independent variables	Battery of word recognition tests	Schonell Reading Ages
Moray House Picture I.Q.	·640	·624
Mental age	·590	·596
Sex	·065	·017
NON LETTER TESTS		
a. Recognition of a visual symbol	·399	·406
b. Recognition of a visual series	·616	·567
c. Identification of rhymes	·476	·491
d. Identification of similar initial sounds	·686	·582
LETTER AND PICTURE TESTS		
e. Synthesis of visual letter into a word	·715	·597
f. Analysis of initial letter from an oral word	·767	·580
g. Serial orientation of two initial consonants	·867	·760
h. Knowledge of alphabet (visual)	·755	·679
i. Identification of vowel sounds	·744	·573

Correlation between Schonell Reading Ages of whole sample and the Word Recognition original battery: $r = ·883$

Correlation between Reading Ages of 79 junior children and middle 28 items of the final test: $r = ·885$

Correlation between Reading Ages of 79 junior children and full 50 items of final test: $r = ·900$

RESULTS OF FACTOR ANALYSIS (AFTER ROTATIONS BY HAND)
OF THE ORIGINAL BATTERY OF TESTS

	FACTORS		
	I	II	III
NON VERBAL/NON LETTER TESTS			
Memory for visual symbols (a)	·49	·52	·00
Memory for a series of symbols (b)	·68	·53	·04
Combined visual tests (a, b)	·70	·70	—·03
Initial sound association (c)	·68	·37	·27
Rhymes (d)	·54	·22	—·26
Combined visual/aural (a, b, c, d)	·82	·46	—·09
Battery of letter/picture tests (e, f, g, h, i)	·83	·15	·52
SUBTESTS OF ORIGINAL WORD RECOGNITION			
Initial vowels (1)	·77	·09	·44
Initial multiple consonants (2)	·85	—·11	·00
Common word endings (3)	·84	—·29	·00
Vowel combinations (combined vowels) (4)	·87	—·11	·15
Irregular ("sight") words (5)	·75	—·04	·23
Regular ("phonic") three letter words (6)	·84	—·08	·35
Combined Word Recognition Battery (1-6)	·94	—·12	·20
Schonell Reading Age	·89	—·14	—·02
Picture I.Q. (Moray House 7+)	·66	·00	·00
Mental Age	·60	·41	—·24
Sex (girls)	·13	—·83	·00

FINAL TEST
Split half (odd even) reliability: r = ·954
Correlation between main 28 items,
    and 22 easier and difficult items: r = ·908
Kuder Richardson (Formula 20): r = ·983

Sample of 168 retarded readers taking remedial education
Correlation between Burt Word Reading
    Ages and final *Word Recognition Test:* r = ·823
Mean Burt Reading Age: 6y 10m
Mean score WRT: 37·8
Standard deviation of Burt ages: 14 months
Standard deviation of *Word Recognition Test* scores: 9·9